The Rise Of Judge Felicia, A Vow Against Injustice

Sibongiseni Masengemu

Published by Sibongiseni Masengemu, 2025.

THE RISE OF JUDGE FELICIA, A VOW AGAINST INJUSTICE

First edition. August 11, 2025.

ISBN: 979-8231676989

Written by Sibongiseni Masengemu.

Table of Contents

CHAPTER 1: THE LAST JOURNEY

Felicia watched the world blur by from the train window, a kaleidoscope of green fields and distant, unfamiliar towns. Her mother hummed a gentle tune beside her, her hand resting warmly on Felicia's head. Across from them, her father pointed to a flock of birds taking flight, their wings a sudden splash of black against the bright sky. He smiled, a deep, full smile that made the corners of his eyes crinkle. Felicia was ten years old, and this trip was an adventure.

The train rattled along the tracks, a rhythmic, comforting song. It was a sound that had filled her life with the promise of new sights and smells, of grand stations and hidden cities. It was the sound of her family, together, exploring a new country.

Then came the silence. Not a peaceful quiet, but a sudden, jarring emptiness. The gentle rhythm stopped. The hum from her mother's lips ceased. A sharp, metallic screech ripped through the air, followed by a violent lurch that sent everything flying. Felicia was thrown against the seat, then against the floor. A cacophony of breaking glass and screaming filled the carriage, a chorus of terror that drowned out all other sound.

She didn't see her parents after that. Not really. She saw fragments—her mother's bright floral dress torn at the hem, her father's shoe lying forgotten near a pile of rubble. She was lifted from the wreckage by a stranger with a kind face, but she felt no comfort. She was just a little girl, holding a small, stuffed toy with a missing eye, surrounded by a language she didn't understand, and the crushing weight of a silence that was colder and sharper than any sound.

CHAPTER 2: THE NEW NORMAL

The orphanage was a place of muted colors and hushed sounds. The walls were a pale, peeling yellow, and the floors were so worn they no longer creaked under the weight of the many children who lived there. Felicia, wrapped in a blanket that smelled faintly of old linens and disinfectant, felt like a ghost. She was ten years old, but felt a century older. The other children, with their games and their laughter, seemed to belong to a world she had left behind forever. She watched them from a distance, her small stuffed toy clutched tight in her arms, its single glass eye a silent companion.

Days blurred into weeks. She learned a few words of the new language, but she found herself unable to speak. The words felt foreign and heavy, like stones in her throat. The matron, a stern but not unkind woman, would bring her meals and try to coax her to talk, but Felicia would only stare, her eyes reflecting a loss that was too big for a child's heart. Her parents' faces, once so clear and full of life, were beginning to fade, becoming soft, watercolor memories she was afraid to lose.

One afternoon, the matron sat beside her on the small bed. Her face was different—less stern, more hesitant. "Felicia," she said, her voice gentle and slow. "There are people who want to meet you. A family."

Felicia didn't react. The words were a soft, meaningless buzzing in her ears. She looked at her toy, then back at the matron. "A family," the woman repeated, trying to catch her gaze. "They want to take you home."

Home. The word was a knife's edge, sharp and cold. It brought with it a flood of images: the warm train car, her mother's humming, her father's smiling eyes. A place she could never go back to. She felt a tremor run through her body, but she remained still. She was no longer a little girl who cried; she was a statue, carved from the cold, hard memory of a train wreck.

CHAPTER 3: A NEW FAMILY

The woman had a kind face, round and soft, with eyes that crinkled at the corners when she smiled. She wore a purple dress with white flowers on it, and her voice was as gentle as a lullaby. Felicia felt her hand being held, a warmth she hadn't felt in what felt like a lifetime. "My name is Laura," the woman said, her voice a soothing balm. "And this is my husband, Thomas."

The man, Thomas, stood beside her. He was tall and thin, with a face like a stone wall. His hands were clasped behind his back, and his eyes, a cold, hard blue, seemed to look right through Felicia, not at her. When he spoke, it was a short, sharp grunt, and he didn't offer his hand. Felicia felt a shiver of unease, a small, dark cloud settling over her heart. The matron, ever cheerful, tried to bridge the gap with a bright smile. "Felicia, this is your new family."

Felicia looked from the kind woman to the cold man, then down at her old shoes. She was an object, a broken thing being chosen from a shelf. She was not a little girl going home; she was a possession being acquired. The ride in the car was a blur of silence, with Laura trying to make conversation and Thomas staring out the window, his jaw set in a hard line. When they arrived at the house, a large, cold structure with perfectly manicured lawns, Laura helped her out of the car. Thomas went inside without a word.

The house was not a home. It was a museum of cold perfection, and Felicia felt more alone than ever. That night, as she lay in a bed that was too big and too soft, she heard his voice, a low rumble from the next room. She couldn't understand the words, but the tone was enough.

It was a sound like breaking glass, sharp and full of hidden anger. She clutched her toy, its single eye a lonely star in the dark, and knew that the storm had just begun.

CHAPTER 4: THE STORM WITHIN

The museum of a house became Felicia's prison. Weeks turned into months, each one a colorless repetition of the last. Thomas's presence was a constant, looming threat. His anger wasn't a sudden storm but a low-pressure system that settled over the house, making the air thick and heavy. His punishments were small at first—a sharp word for a misplaced book, a slap for a scuff on the perfect white floor. They were never in front of Laura, but always when she had her back turned, or when she was in another room.

Laura, for her part, was a master of avoidance. She would fill the silence with a stream of cheerful chatter, telling Felicia stories about her own childhood or describing the elaborate dinner parties she planned. If she saw a shadow on Felicia's cheek or a bruise on her arm, she would pretend not to. She would change the subject, or offer a sweet cookie, her eyes filled with a fleeting look of pity that quickly vanished. One afternoon, after Thomas had grabbed her arm so hard her fingers turned white, Felicia went to Laura. "He hurt me," she said, the words a raw whisper. Laura's soft face hardened. "Thomas has a temper," she said, her voice brittle. "You must learn to be more careful. He is a good man, he just gets frustrated. You're a part of our family now, and families have to be patient with each other."

The words hit harder than any slap. Felicia retreated to her room, a fortress of cold comfort. In the quiet, she began to remember what she had heard her father talk about before the accident—the laws of the land, the rights of the individual. She didn't know the words for it, but she knew that what was happening was wrong. She had nowhere to go, no one to tell, but a seed of defiance was planted. She would find a way to make it stop. She would report them. It was a terrifying, impossible thought for a child, but it was a thought that kept her from shattering completely. It was the first flicker of the fire that would one day forge the judge.

CHAPTER 5: AN UNHEARD PLEA

The courthouse was a grand, intimidating building, all sharp angles and unforgiving stone. Felicia felt a terror far greater than any she had known at home. With a borrowed pencil and a small piece of paper, she had scrawled a few simple sentences in her new, halting language. He hits me. My mother does not help. I am afraid. She clutched the note like a life raft.

Inside, she was a tiny figure lost in a sea of adults in dark suits. A woman with glasses and a tight bun behind a desk looked down at her with a tired smile. Felicia held out the note, her hand trembling. The woman took it, her smile fading as she read the words. She led Felicia to a small, dusty office where a man with a tired face sat. He read the note, then looked at her with an expression she couldn't place—was it pity? Distrust?

He spoke to her in a low, gentle voice, asking questions she couldn't fully answer. He asked for proof, for witnesses. Felicia could only shake her head. "They are my parents," she said in a whisper, her new words feeling clumsy and small. "They are a good family," he said, and the words were like a heavy door slamming shut. He told her that children sometimes misunderstood, that families had their own ways. He told her to go home.

As she walked out into the blinding sunlight, Felicia felt the last vestiges of hope drain from her. The man had not seen her. He had not heard her. She was invisible. She had done everything she could, and it was not enough. The seed of defiance that had been planted earlier in her room now took root, hardening into a core of unyielding resolve.

She realized that she could not rely on others for justice. She would have to become the kind of person who could make sure pleas like hers were never ignored again. She would have to become the law itself.

CHAPTER 6: THE UNBREAKABLE RESOLVE

The courthouse had been a lesson, a harsh, unforgiving truth. Justice, Felicia learned, was not something to be handed to her, but something she would have to build for herself. She returned to the cold house, no longer with a quiet hope, but with a simmering fire in her belly.

From that day on, everything changed. The abuse continued—the harsh words, the swift slaps, the constant expectation of flawless obedience—but Felicia's mind was no longer there. It was in a world of numbers, of histories, of words. Her schoolbooks became her armor. She stayed up late, hunched over a flickering desk lamp, devouring every page, every lesson, every problem. Thomas's voice, raised in anger, became a distant noise. The tears she once cried in her bed at night were replaced by the quiet scratch of a pencil on paper.

Laura would sometimes peer into the room, a confused expression on her face. "You're studying so hard," she'd say, her voice a little too cheerful. "Don't you want to come and watch TV?" Felicia would offer a silent, unblinking shake of her head and go back to her work. She was no longer a little girl looking for a mother's comfort; she was a student on a mission. Her grades soared. Teachers, once concerned by her quiet demeanor, now praised her for her intelligence and focus.

She was a ghost in the house, a body that moved from the dinner table to her room, but her spirit was already a thousand miles away, in a future she was building brick by brick. Every difficult math problem she solved, every historical date she memorized, felt like a small victory. They were proof that her mind was her own, and that no one could take away what she knew. It was a secret, quiet power she was cultivating, and she knew, with the certainty of a child who had lost everything, that it would one day make her unstoppable.

CHAPTER 7: THE ESCAPE

The high school graduation was a blur of black gowns and bright smiles. Felicia sat among her peers, a silent observer of the boisterous celebration. Her name was called, and she walked across the stage to a polite smattering of applause, a quiet but brilliant star in a galaxy of noise. She was awarded a scholarship to a prestigious university, a detail that was read aloud for everyone to hear. Thomas and Laura sat in the back row, their faces unreadable, but Felicia knew what the scholarship meant. It was not just an award; it was a one-way ticket.

That evening, she packed a single suitcase. She didn't own much, and the things she did have were mostly her books. Laura hovered in the doorway, wringing her hands. "We're so proud of you, Felicia," she said, her voice thin and full of an unspoken apology. "We always knew you would do great things." Felicia looked at her, at the woman who had watched and done nothing. She said nothing in return, the words a bitter lump in her throat.

When Thomas arrived home, he saw her by the door, suitcase in hand. He simply grunted, then stepped around her. He said not a single word of congratulations or farewell. It was the most fitting goodbye she could have imagined. As she stepped out the door and a taxi pulled up to the curb, she felt the oppressive weight of the house lift from her shoulders. The air outside was cool and clean, and she took a deep, shuddering breath. It was the first time she had felt truly free since that train ride so many years ago.

The university campus was a world of its own—sprawling green lawns, old brick buildings, and the excited chatter of new students.

Felicia found her dorm room, a small space with a single bed and a desk, and felt a profound sense of peace. This was her space. Her future. The difficult past, a ghost that had haunted her for so long, felt miles away, and for the first time, she allowed herself a small, hesitant smile. The real work had only just begun.

CHAPTER 8: THE PATH FORWARD

Felicia thrived in the quiet solitude of her dorm room and the vibrant chaos of the campus library. The university wasn't just a place to study; it was a sanctuary. The professors spoke of great thinkers and grand ideas, and no one ever looked at her with pity or distrust. Her mind, once a fortress against abuse, was now free to wander and learn. She found herself drawn to classes that dealt with power, with justice, and with the way societies are built and broken.

It was a lecture on the history of law that solidified her path. The professor, an elderly woman with a sharp mind and an even sharper wit, was discussing the concept of an impartial judiciary. "The law," she said, her voice echoing in the lecture hall, "is not a collection of rules. It is a promise. A promise that every single person, no matter their station in life, will be heard. That no one is above it, and no one is beneath it."

Felicia felt a jolt of recognition. She remembered the tired, dismissive face of the man in the courthouse, and the deafening silence of Laura's complicity. They had failed to keep that promise for her. The law had been a heavy door slammed in her face. In that moment, sitting in a crowded lecture hall, Felicia made a silent vow. She wouldn't just study the law; she would become a keeper of its promise. She would become a judge, a figure of absolute impartiality, a person who could ensure that no child's plea was ever ignored again.

She began to focus her studies, dedicating herself to legal theory and political science with a fervor that amazed her peers. The difficult past, which she had tried to leave behind, was now the fuel for her future. It was no longer a source of shame but a wellspring of purpose. She had a new goal, a new north star, and she would work with an unyielding determination to reach it.

CHAPTER 9: THE SHAPENING OF A BLADE

Law school was a different kind of challenge. The competition was fierce, the hours were long, and the subject matter was dense and unforgiving. But for Felicia, it felt less like a struggle and more like a calling. She absorbed legal precedents and constitutional arguments like a sponge, her mind a finely tuned instrument. While her classmates saw it as a path to power and wealth, Felicia saw it as a set of tools—a new language with which she could finally speak, a set of keys to unlock the doors that had been closed to her as a child.

She became known in her classes for her unwavering resolve. In a mock trial, a classmate argued that a defendant's emotional state should be a factor in sentencing, a plea for mercy based on circumstance. The class murmured in agreement. But Felicia stood up, her voice clear and strong. "Emotion is a factor for a psychologist," she said, her eyes fixed on the professor. "But justice cannot be built on emotion. It must be built on the impartial application of the law. If we allow emotion to sway us, we fail to protect those who are truly voiceless, because their pleas are too easily dismissed."

Her words stunned the room into silence. The professor, a man known for his cynicism, simply nodded. Felicia knew she had alienated some of her peers. She didn't care. Her mission was not to be liked, but to be right. Her past was not a weakness she needed to hide; it was the foundation of her strength. She wasn't just learning to be a lawyer; she was learning to be a judge—uncompromising, fair, and utterly dedicated to the promise of the law.

After three years of relentless work, she graduated at the top of her class. As she walked across the stage to receive her diploma, the applause was not just for her academic achievement, but for the fierce, unshakeable integrity she had already demonstrated. Her education was complete, and she was now ready to enter the world, not as a victim, but as a warrior.

CHAPTER 10: THE FIRST CASE

Felicia landed a job at a small, no-nonsense law firm known for its tenacity. The partners were a hardened lot, a mix of old-school lawyers who respected hard work and young, ambitious associates who saw every case as a rung on a ladder. Felicia was different. She saw every case as a promise to be kept. She worked tirelessly, spending late nights in the office, surrounded by stacks of legal briefs and dusty books. She wasn't chasing money or prestige; she was searching for the truth, one case at a time.

Her first major case was a pro bono assignment. A young, single mother was being evicted from her home by a large, powerful landlord who had been deliberately letting the building fall into disrepair, hoping to force the low-income tenants out. The case was a bureaucratic nightmare, full of loopholes and legal fine print that most lawyers would have considered unwinnable. It was the kind of case that reminded Felicia of her own past—a voiceless person up against a system designed to ignore them.

She dove into the details with an almost obsessive focus. She found every housing code violation, every missed repair order, every lie the landlord had told. When she stood in court, she was not just a young lawyer; she was a force of nature. She spoke not with theatrics, but with a quiet, unshakeable certainty. She presented her evidence with precision, her arguments like a series of hammer blows, each one landing with a devastating, undeniable logic. The opposing counsel, a seasoned veteran of such cases, was visibly rattled.

The judge, a stern woman with a reputation for fairness, looked from Felicia to the landlord's lawyer, then back again. In the end, there was no choice but to rule in Felicia's favor. The tenants were allowed to stay, and the landlord was forced to make the necessary repairs. As Felicia walked out of the courtroom, the young mother hugged her, her eyes filled with tears of gratitude. Felicia simply nodded, a small, weary smile on her face. The win was not a cause for celebration; it was a promise fulfilled. From that day on, her reputation began to grow. She was known as the lawyer who didn't back down, the one who fought for those without a voice, and the legal community began to take notice.

CHAPTER 11: THE CALL

Felicia's reputation wasn't built on flash, but on bedrock. She became known as the lawyer who was not only brilliant but unshakeable. Her integrity was her most potent weapon. She didn't play games or engage in backroom deals. She simply presented the truth, and she did it with such clarity and force that she was impossible to ignore. Senior partners in other firms began to fear her, and judges, who had seen it all, began to respect her. Her name, once whispered in the halls of the courthouse, now carried the weight of authority.

Her work on pro bono cases earned her a special kind of renown. The story of the young mother she had saved from eviction was just the first of many. She took on cases of neglect, of abuse, of power used to silence the powerless. The legal community began to notice that Felicia was not just practicing law; she was living it. She was fulfilling the promise of justice, one person at a time. Her work was so exemplary that her name was mentioned in national news stories and legal journals.

One day, while working late in her office, her phone rang. The number was unfamiliar. She answered, expecting a client. Instead, a calm, professional voice on the other end introduced herself as an aide to the President of the country. Felicia felt her blood run cold. She waited, her heart pounding a heavy rhythm against her ribs.

"The President has been following your career," the aide said. "He is very impressed with your dedication to justice and your impeccable record. He believes you are exactly the kind of person who should be serving on the bench. He would like to offer you a position as a judge."

Felicia sat there for a long moment, the words sinking into her very bones. The child who had been silenced in a dusty courthouse office, the girl who had been dismissed and ignored, was now being offered a chance to command that very space. It was not a victory for her ego, but a profound and sobering responsibility. She thought of the little girl with the missing-eyed toy, and of the many children like her. Her voice, when she finally spoke, was steady and sure. "I accept," she said.

ABOUT AN AUTHOR

Sibongiseni Masengemu is an author known for writing thought-provoking and emotionally charged books that explore themes of motherhood, resilience, love, and self-discovery. Here are some key facts about the author and their works:

Books by Sibongiseni Masengemu

- **Unstoppable Mama: Motherhood Redefined**: This memoir tells the story of the author's journey as a young mother, navigating the challenges of parenthood and finding strength in vulnerability. The book explores themes of unconditional love, perseverance, and transformation.
- **My Resurrection**: Although details about this book are limited, it is listed among Masengemu's works on ThriftBooks.
- **Confession Of A Lost Soul**: Another title by Masengemu that explores themes of self-discovery and introspection.
- **The Unseen Architects: The Calculated Redemption**: This book appears to be a work of fiction that explores themes of justice, redemption, and power struggles.
- **Beyond the Book's**: This eBook explores the intersection of science, philosophy, and spirituality, offering insights into the human condition and the universe [1] [2] [3].

Writing Style and Themes

Masengemu's writing style is characterized by raw honesty, vulnerability, and a deep exploration of the human experience. The author's works often touch on themes of:

- **Motherhood and Parenting**: Masengemu writes about the challenges and triumphs of motherhood, highlighting the importance of resilience and perseverance.
- **Self-Discovery and Introspection**: The author's works encourage readers to reflect on their own experiences and emotions, promoting a deeper understanding of oneself and the world.
- **Love and Relationships**: Masengemu explores the complexities of human relationships, emphasizing the importance of love, forgiveness, and compassion.

DEDICATION

"To those who've been marginalized, oppressed, or silenced,
May these pages amplify your voice,
Validate your struggles,
And fuel the fight for justice.
May your stories be heard,
Your truths be told,
And your resilience inspire a brighter future.
This book is a testament to the power of the human spirit,
A beacon of hope in the darkest moments,
And a reminder that even in the face of adversity,
Your voice matters, your story deserves to be told,
And your fight for justice is worth every step.
May we rise together,
Unite in our pursuit of equality,
And create a world where every voice is heard,
Every story is valued,
And every soul is treated with dignity."

Don't miss out!

Visit the website below and you can sign up to receive emails whenever Sibongiseni Masengemu publishes a new book. There's no charge and no obligation.

https://books2read.com/r/B-A-LADUC-HIWTG

BOOKS 2 READ

Connecting independent readers to independent writers.

www.ingramcontent.com/pod-product-compliance
Lightning Source LLC
LaVergne TN
LVHW022327200926
848481LV00004B/1449